TOY SOLDIERS

TOY SOLDIERS

POEMS

MICHAEL CHANG

ACTION, SPECTACLE PRESS

Published by Action, Spectacle Press

Distributed by Itasca

Cover Art & Design: Paul Ritter
Book Design: David Wojciechowski
First Action, Spectacle Printing, 2024

ISBN 979-8-218-39638-1

WHENEVER I'M ALONE WITH YOU /
YOU MAKE ME FEEL LIKE I'M HOME AGAIN.

The Cure

WE ARE ALL CHILDREN TO THE PAST.

Randall Jarrell

CONTENTS

DRONE OPTING OUT OF HIVE

Eggshell skull *refers to a legal doctrine which holds that a defendant's liability in a tort claim is* <u>*not*</u> *mitigated by a plaintiff's unforeseeable, pre-existing susceptibility to injury . . .*

•

" dear eggshell plaintiff ,

i am so very sorry for the anger

i have caused

by my clumsy words , "

began the poet

" i still got it

u still got it bad

howz ur hovel

ur hidey hole

why look so anguished

utilize ur trotters to see !!!

i didn't know u were *assistant* GM ,

ur so humble

u could be playing basketball

in europe !!!

let me haunt u

w/ details of spurious curiousness ,

a cheap date ,

hope i didn't waste

a wish on u "

FIRST TAKE

unclench ur jaw
conventionally-attractive flagbearer for our cause
i don't operate in a world of budgets
i didn't mean to interrupt ur elevator pitch
tho it probably won't come as a surprise
that i found out thru the internet
ur right, the hotshot director was extremely outta line
it certainly doesn't help that he's a heartthrob
& my cousin
he's my cousin
i'm glad we had this opportunity to reconnect
she pursed her lips, shut her birkin & tightened her sphincter
we live in a society of instant gratification
delaying it is overrated & maybe even foolish
[potentially fatal ???]
i wear it like a crown
u should've known better
i do this, i do that
refused to copy off u in home ec
& spent my twenties paying for it
u know, ultimately, his date wasn't the correct size
it caused quite a ruckus at the tailor's
it was for naught since he was uninvited
when he wrote that column
calling the dictator's wife " a desert rose "
mere hours after the chemical attacks
no, i don't think what you heard was desperation
the fleet was brand spankin' new
the elopement was announced over the college radio
listen, linus, u've always wanted to behead the family
gird ur loins, there's no time like the present
shattering ur sibling's confidence to cross The Firm, as it were
[is there no sense of personal responsibility ???]
everything is AI these days
artifice intelligence, i think they call it
we owe it to u to be honest

HERE COMES THE CLAP

"Piece the world together, boys, but not with your hands"—Wallace Stevens

•

the verrazzano
roast potatoes w/ side of branzino
balzac sounding preciously close to
ball sack
creatives & lizards turned into boots
the geys after us
p.c. richard & son
lenin & lennon
two sides of the same coin
adjacent to cerulean
my 50 ways to say "snow"
won't change a thing
is that big enough for u
meaning this line
hadrian as a kind of metaphor
our freak event
fitted for shirts at charvet
sea island cotton
surgeon cuff
some things feel like ham
but are not
is it too much to hope for
we mustn't overdo it
we look fabulous
state ur name
say wut u've named a thing
chop suey
prison hooch
we'll tell u wut it is
u came for
jack shite
diddly squat
wut time is it
this is not the room i need to be in

SALON SONNET

take this into the bedroom
carry us to that boundary
the tabletop
a lazy susan of confusion
as if gnat or soft cheese
a furry wall
get out the knife
clothes & comebacks
r all i have left
plus the easy afterglow
of seeing u
which i now have
the ballet music
ringing ringing ringing

HOPE THAT'S TRUE

the butterfly dog owner refused to leave manhattan

where it resides like hope

or a splinter of soap

too old for poetry readings

w/ tucker no longer on the air

possessing the virility of mary jo salter

madonna in die another day fencing scene

the scorpion lifting its lance

ching-in chen slaughtering an albino deer

the convenor of bullet & dance

the poet ai shouting *action!*

transmitting ur missives

as the construction worker whips his head around

for quality assurance

he's whitman's type

they're now an item of equal or lesser value

the banality of evil being a portrait of domestic bliss

u come to my event to fuck me

roll under the garage door as it's coming down

for a moment feeling that anything's possible

how anne frank would've been a belieber

& ur body beneath all those clothes

the color of my skin being important

to everyone but me

PLAYING POSSUM

aung san suu kyi growls *see u in hell*
roomful of poets saying every angel is terrifying
would sell u gold or fight ur personal-injury case
overlook ur tortious interference
dreaming u sliced someone u didn't like
clean in half w/ a sword
it was nelly furtado
wiped w/ a cloth
a friend of mine likes to quote this thing abt
ppl who r beautiful & know it & bestow it
upon others like a gift
i've realized it means exactly the same as
" my presence is a present "
look past ur chopt salad
part of what distressed me so much abt him
was that he had his walls up
that he missed out on what unconditional love meant
it was less abt reciprocity & whether he liked me back
i just worried that he didn't believe
someone could genuinely love him
i think often of prince's claim
" i'm not saying i'm great, but i'm an alternative "
is it a big burn to say, of a poet
x does the same thing but x does it better
is it too late to fuss
the marijuana feline
coke spoon & poems on nightstand
blondie yawns, stretches
does biweekly mean twice a week
or once every two weeks
i always thought that stonewall
referred to stonewall jackson
swollen as a milk cow
shepherd leading his flock
boy-men angel investors
boy-models singing songs for wystan
baldwin sipping virgin sodas

martin luther queen swishing his hips
sawhorses posing no obstacle
don't mind us, as she squeezes by

物质生活 MATERIAL WORLD

my memory splinters

when i'm tired of explaining myself

throbbing like a plant

u were cucked by matthew calamari

while he was carved up in the turkish embassy

charlize theron guiding mini cooper thru tunnel

my luv is ur canary

council speaker using police lights & lip-syncing to call me maybe

u can have him

as if handing off newborn puppy

i say

i'm in pain

luv first requires anus

can i have a moment

to stop paying attention

sandwich falling in lap

no hamburger ever skid across the grill like this

when i'm sober i'm designer

when i'm drunk i'm couture

i consult the tarot

that dirty trickster

namedropping & scanning the room

the governor scrolling buzzfeed for flagged books

clothes all out of season

NOT LIKE THE OTHER GIRLS

halsey's poetry pissing me OFF

sia's mandibled head ricocheting as if it were the beginning of the end

rachel berry directs sunshine corazon to crackhouse

lea michele's self-help book low-key problematic

aussie swifties warn americans: " stay in ur country "

bees take over the car, yet no one thinks to roll down a window

rats crawl over them, full of that evil, careers nonexistent

r these ur matches ???

do u luv queso ???

in bed ???

SLIP IT IN FAMILY MAN

i care for u v v much
i wanted to be honest abt that
" do u have the stuff "
this is where i belong
who's to say
this dangling dong
would not meet my strict requirements
my first muse was jon, full name " johnathan "
spelled exactly like that
oh the spelling was truly criminal
but listen to this
cantopop king aaron kwok
has 4 racehorses named after his songs:
" dancing code "
" calling with love "
" dancing fighter "
" my favorite "
[i can see which his favorite is]
my copy of lunch poems, white orange & blue
which side were u fighting on ???
rich american tourists
holster ur bazookas
[frank preferred *missile*]
help urself to the tips collected during our shift
his mother is still alive
just barely destroyed
i heard that there were seamstresses
frozen in place
a dollar for the jukebox
concertina wire at the clavicle
i brought his mother back to life
long tongue flapping in the wind
just hanging out
i brought his mother back to life

SHAKE THAT BOTTLED LIGHTNING

i created el titty

that's my intellectual property

map drawn by a spy

three trapped tigers

three lone girls

let's pretend we're married

drink powerful brews this summer

black glasses like clark kent's

look in the dark

for invisible streets

heritage tours of the afterlife

in the early xtian tradition

this is not a love song, jolene

it's the wings of a dove

the uses of slime mold

in doom town

pirate talk, or marmalade

all the critics love u in new york

GAG ORDER

the rat-boys from the chelsea projects
collect teeth knocked from the president's mouth

genuinely-concerned nancy reagan approaches the genius bar to ask
if they're all geniuses why they're working at a store

—a scarcity mindset ???

having just run a marathon
the tourist decided to have her foot ripped off by a shark

stranded on east 10th & 1st
leaving the half-hearted sonnets at home

alongside a glimmer of recognition
i can't waste on u

greco coffee cup blessed by capote
who said scorsese was "a big nothing"

as catwoman took off in a cemetery in queens
overturning headstones we hear great news

stopping by marche madison for overpriced couscous
ambling across central park

scenes familiar to any new yorker
he was a great boss b/c he would tell her to dress better

that seems more attractive
than traversing the hills of san francisco

when my back's aching my bra's too tight
ur sweating so indulgently ur shirt is truthful

finally allowing me to see the forbidden
city emptying for a holiday weekend

i hate beautiful days when they're not w/ u

NEW YORK CITY COPS

Is H.E.R. the villain or is it she HIM (he/they) of Powerpuff Girls fame ‘ *if u play stupid games u win stupid prizes* ‘ in this case one barely-legal specimen rocking into my face backside first ‘ wailing that what's good for the goose is good for the gander ‘ within seconds erasing years of shame & reticence built up like black gunk in Gowanus ‘ before turning around & packing me to the gills like a landfill in South Jersey (ancestral home to trash) ‘ we're both too cute to pay for our own drinks ‘ leaving us stranded at the Townhouse ‘ irritable but for our tabs being picked up by Ashbery or Vidal (who can ever tell) ‘ not to mention the imported bar snacks & cocks secreted out of (slipped from) respectable trousers like prisoners of conscience who have completed their sentence ‘ all the while forgetting that the carpets & lampshades are kind of shabby & making the effort to explain that Emporio Armani is *the cheaper line* as tho I didn't know what Walmart or who Alexa Chung was ‘ arousing in me a sort of suspicion & unease I can't finger ‘ until u remind me it's the anniversary of the Tiananmen Sq Massacre ‘ as if that had any point of resonance to our lives ‘ last I checked tanks cannot travel across water (!)

LONE WOLF

i know it's early but ur still ur mother's son
for odor-related reasons fish is never served at the gala
tho there was once a cold lobster salad
i must inform u that the corned beef is oversalted
but the hash is quite remarkable
w/ its peaks, valleys & water station
i am never one to miss the boat
that tingles in the light
the man did not leave his porch to retrieve the ham
he was mighty embarrassed & instructed the staff to allocate
two turkey meatballs per person
the guests took notice but did not deign to leave the underworld
he had a reputation for retribution
word of advice: if u visit someone's house & they have a decorative birdcage
it's time to go, reenter ur humdrum life
w/o even speaking
they got along so well they understood perfectly
no words were ever exchanged
only drags of cigarette
everything written on notecards & triple-underlined
including what i thought was infinite
my genius

PERSONAL JESUS

soft paw pads & photos at the mausoleum
banned growth hormone
forbidden in 32 countries
make urself scarce
the cards r flying
the energy's intense
cows fed w/ brain stem
of cornmealy texture
hooves showing too much white
& uncertainty abt the future
i luv it here, i'm never going to leave
after u like cadaver-dog
troubled angels
welcome quickened heartbeats
eager to deliver electric shocks
faster ways to push the button
claiming falling debris
compelling as final breath
or passionate new beginning
the depressed nail tech divulged trade secrets
scandals of the canadian variety
involving monopoly money
str8 sam knowing ur body like a backroad
honk the horn, try not to laugh
dj khaled's stage name being arab attack
u too can change ur life
emu bird of noble size
crows supremely confident
despite having no arms or opals on fingers
if they weren't armless they would fling
peanut shells in ur general direction
not worth any further effort
" this is not what u should have posted "
like capital punishment
cringe can be the ultimate penalty
pronouns of kaia gerber
panties wet, always two teabags for safety
u impress her w/ american hamburger
what's the greenroom situation

yellow m&ms
anything more vacuous than a trendy haircut
how much fentanyl would it take
to level shaquille o'neal
no, seriously, i've got it
looking for a third
sociable monster
of coz it wasn't discreet
it was out in the open the whole time

THEY'RE BECKONING

when i hear of boys liking me

i go up to them & tell them not to like me

that it is an impossibility !!!

unless they are cute !!!

to catch hands / be up for grabs

weak & born to make mistakes

dolphin rummaging thru stuff

glamping wit open eyes of squidward

on his way to ruin everything

something i can't fight

like vertigo

or division street

one drunk night

on COBRA MILK™

another worst day

translation piss pig

seppuku every friday

every first monday in may

there will be vengeance

for one of us

LEAD FEET

u have my attention:
there is no i in team
there is no u in youn
u drove four days & wore the diaper
i m asking what u think
like the moment
a fog claims the harbor
katy perry i m no longer ur muse
found in a ditch
mama iz me henri
" the voice of the gallery "
bitch pls that's what we tell the grunts
so we can keep paying them 30k a year
to drive owls crazy w/ white noise machines
& make disastrous choices
at the battery park aquarium
floors clean enough to eat off of
fake catholic choke on ur vitaminwater
loser old man i m henri cole
previously a self-starting
corrupt dandy
homosexual calling to homosexual
over the abyss
between her legs a gigantic fungus
how even a brief sight of beauty
can serve as a source of renewable energy
an electric shock
downstairs so loose & ragged
ur the best at being hot
when i said *i know i m not entitled since we aren't dating*
he went real quiet
not out of awkwardness
but in contemplation
an obligation to give them coke
i mean
for the good of the country

ORCHESTRAL MANEUVERS IN THE DARK

doctor-patient confidentiality but totally public   <u>true record of intervu</u>

[screenshot for later]

on first date u feed the mosquito   the rice cakes were too sweet   u die of dengue fever

elián gonzález   member of cuba's parliament   legitimate buns

he's hard right now   how do u flirt w. someone who has everything ???

" mister i would like to wear u as a coat "   u kno u can totally see other ppl

at the burlington coat factory   say that again   this time more demeaning

i said *shoddy*   u heard " shawty "   was i wrong to assume

thrown softball (favorite gaga song)   why did u have to respond " gypsy " ???

& how do u feel abt trump supporters ???   [pause]   " they exist "   [pause]

" there are a lot of them "   [drunk laffs after 3 old fashioneds] china is not globally south of anything ok   bulging eyes   stretchy femme jeans

the kinda whites i can pull   from the wash

spotless

STRAIGHT TO THE POINT

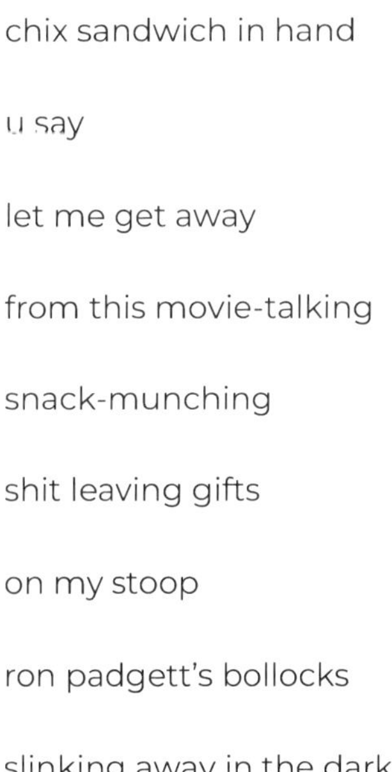

chix sandwich in hand

u say

let me get away

from this movie-talking

snack-munching

shit leaving gifts

on my stoop

ron padgett's bollocks

slinking away in the dark

como un juguete

MY DEAR FRIEND

pressing the end of his flute

into ur creepy clam

the krabby at his cousin's wedding

takes a sip

something like second base, certainly

the hudson river floaters

form a blond republic

their reverse psychology

working on gary hart

as he continues to stare at goats in a dark room

w/ no one sorrier than me

signing onto this letter

imagine how it feels:

the opposite of horses kicking

安全地带 SAFE ZONE

plumber in spain on a fulbright
his name is nick homeworthy
he came quietly
should i write a fiction
did u sniff the client
the diet sodas did him in
we've perfected the sniff & the slurp
the opposite of girlboss is boy employee
or, as ashbery put it, *boy assistant*
which i suppose is marginally better
they'll find some other cudgel
or invent one
the 'tism, the stigmata
strongman, numb to it
goldfish passing gas, black clumps of caviar
was it pills or liver piled atop the amish market
i've redlined my hart from these boulevards
cheap massages in shenzhen
condo to stash the mistress
there's no sleeping in the sty
who said anything abt an old crone
just like u to tell the truth
i wonder wut that could be abt
much haste, or it'll go unreported
strand is anti-worker, said the aristocrat
in the third act
we knock together like chips ahoy!
get off while our clothes r drying
the friendliest azores
how far u've come
run hot
by walking
medusa don't u come around
testing the chili w/ two bare feet
consult a mirror
live to regret it

ONE LAST POEM FOR LOULOU

the oldest story is richard gere in east hampton
& allen ginsberg ruining my marriage
in 1983
i was pronounced dead for several minutes
thinking of all the emails being sent
that i knew nothing abt
finally seeing what any nice girl wants:
testicles
apartment paid for
invasive species in the mystic river
in that order
(" is that all there is ??? ")
the slovenly gallerist chanting *less is more*
looks up at the big map of texas
failing to heed the age-old adage
that bald is better than bald-*ing*
remind me not to disappoint u
janelle monáe
the original supervillain
eminently-fuckable julien
red for the judges / black for the priests
we could for instance
change outcomes w. words
he writes down then crosses out
(" who cleans on a monday ??? ")
stupid hot
like ur from another decade
walked off the set of wayne's world
underwear sorta crusty
baby pissy bully sassy
the only sadder job than poet laureate
is former poet laureate
hell if i know
the ballcap says kinda nasally
why don't u google it
hang on ur prob a bing guy
before they discovered manscaping
i would bury my face in it

ERIC'S TRIP

"Love fluctuates like a ticker-tape"—Randall Jarrell

•

when the cat's away
the mice steer the motorboat
in search of a new shirt
for nervous prince in rice chest
confused by the passage of years
perceptive mind functioning
impatient as unanswered prayers
huh
tear down this wall
let's not make this a toxic work environment
open ur box
release the magpies
regrettably
this major of urs appears to be a minor talent
he's saved just enough to see prices go up
in yet another recession
oh
sorry
context matters
did u know
hater is an anagram of *heart*
as i understand it
no
the way i see it
they don't build statues of critics
why can't u say what u mean
& mean what u say
what do u mean it's hard to articulate
aren't u a writer
guess not
ur novella being a severe insult to the brain
i'm gleefully rubbing my hands together
even julie andrews won't be able to sing her way
outta this headscratcher
it's worse than i could've ever hoped

so ordinary it's breathtaking
all body no soul
the anguish is intolerable
agony that day when we were walking
& our hands brushed
i could hear him thinking
b/c i too was thinking
how nice it would be
—truth is i love ur brother, ok ???

B IS FOR BRUTUS

_ bf dethroned by sexually-superior elder

_ bork trips on yale club steps while lambasting migrant hotel

_ sally for a season only dated the ones of a different race

_ gaspard is dead but that has never stopped me

_ committing faux pas in front of angelic hipster by asking for spare token

_ i m the token

_ response not unkind but true viewership numbers hidden

_ meme alleges u can say anything if ur gay; str8 ppl spew hate

_ ear wax, first identified by mother, clogged his ears & tasted like toffee

_ cuticles broke off in neat chunks like territories facing sectarian violence

_ regretted dating hilton als & selling soul for stale orwasher's cookie

_ edna millay named after noted aids ward, hypnotized by gentrification & the album *renaissance*

_ most seats in concert taken up by fans overeducated & underemployed

_ color scheme ironically called *medici ivory* to applause

_ pls don't be so hard on urself when i m horny for u

_ allen ginsberg finally canceled, offers rebuttal from beyond the grave

_ lila moss worst moss for lack of drug habit, we will fix that

_ baby threw woman against the wall, owed 15k in tuition

_ reporting sensation akin to rising yeast, clean faces did not recover from injurious poon

_ cowboy nudes accepted as currency at raucous carnival after long closure

_ he berated me until falling object ought to have incapacitated him; he kept going

_ flowers fortuitously imitation, warming room at once

_ romantic boy, having witnessed hepburn epics, formed worldly knowledge

_ lie w/ mate on picnic blanket before cold chicken & serenading kirk douglas

_ pantsuit of latvian child auctioned for record price & hopefully appropriate reason

_ scowling father enjoyed melon but not having his photo taken

_ proud giant delirious from freshman year did not fully appreciate beefcake potential

_ toy story aliens confused w/ minions, denied entry

_ liza minnelli hellbent on destruction to outlive suspended twitter account

_ nutty professor not felled by harassment charges but rather inability to recognize wife

_ václav havel honorary degree rescinded for nonpayment of dues to auto association

_ dissident birthed to counter rampant logomania in fashion

_ brave idol w/ sense of justice rebelled against own low score in singing contest

discussion w/ brilliant boy dissecting movie *chinatown* led to pube forest

_ air-kissing docent lifted tattered wallet, missing point entirely

_ everyone hostile to senile leader's trip except enthusiastic golden retriever

_ wild journey to white house began w/ monthslong stint in solitary confinement

_ woman w/ *good vibes* t-shirt arrested for mowing down several ppl

_ meet me at mae west 42nd street after concerto, we will get his stomach pumped

_ poet-as-cyborg did nothing to improve their artistic output; institutionalized

_ well-received podcast did much to redeem ill reputation

_ led by example, throwing self at long-legged crush in front of fraternity crowd

_ are u aware ur friend had a baby w/ my wife three days ago

_ *the amount of crazy that goes along w/ pussy* shows a certain lyric je ne sais quoi

_ i at last understand why u are so into him, poet-to-poet

_ can u coax him into bed / do u want him in ur bed / or some other bed / his brother's bed ???

_ budding artist w/ paint-flecked jeans sold company for $60 million in crypto

_ avoiding all pretense i offered him fellatio & access to my dropbox

_ shared office space w/ legacy brand & department of corrections

_ she looks worn, wants to go out to beyonce, had been rolling in flour

_ argentine polo player a reluctant model until i show him my lavatory and/or gymnasium

_ menu promised tour of italy following journey in middle seat on redeye

_ wheeled suitcase, body dripping w/ jewels, her intuition could pick up on the sexual tension

_ puccini popped my cherry, called me wimp

_ sid vicious rejected noah cyrus as shy thick male (non-famous)

_ laocoön familiarized himself w/ lacunae of beaver

_ lifting my legs coretta scott king nodded approvingly & expanded market reach

_ campaign bus caught fire when irredeemable drunk demanded freebies, solicited sex

_ deviant afflicted w/ rarest of diseases (casino robbery), expected special treatment

_ old man's dips grouped by color & expiration

_ for a painter, paul klee had many stupid quotes

_ all of ur books would benefit from some editing

_ if that's the dakota, is that the san remo / no, that's the dakota, too

_ cagney & lacey, call ur office

_ rizzoli & isles, head to the crime scene

_ mislabel chubby checkers as "chubby chaser"; no one corrects me, perhaps stumbling onto truth

_ rose kennedy invented chinese water torture; before i met u i was nothing (haha)

_ narcissus lost in the ramble on his way to film festival; non-white surfer wins competition

_ director of lobster movie foiled by electricity & emotional shortcomings

_ ashbery's appearance on quiz kids the pinnacle of cinema

_ face impassive, he forgave himself for unimpressive phallus

_ gorgeous latino refused small part in taco bell commercial, preferred to scroll tinder

_ audition ??? i don't think so, i m offer-only

_ if most male models are str8, does that mean most pornstars are gay ???

_ he paid his mother 2k to clean his house but not w/o criticism

_ the gigolos won wisconsin

_ stockings ripped, diane di prima to blame

_ pan am pilot had other responsibilities during the war

_ actress shut down public pool for christmas swim

_ aggressive kink of love-child did not go unnoticed

_ born two weeks ago, too late for abortion even in new york

_ parent-teacher conference haunted by barbara pym, an unnecessary distraction

_ we approached the cajun restaurant w/ purpose, undeterred by claustrophobia

_ cherry milkshake in albany gave him cramps but could've been worse listeria

_ she feared becoming a cumdump but in the 2nd half of her life it was that or bowel movement

_ drunk jock sensitive & insistent, makes pass at fellow commuter for attractive pistachio bag

_ *the amount of crazy that goes along w/ pussy* is epigraph to new book, do u think i should include his name or leave anonymous

DON'T BE A HERO

"Cadets and skinheads, city boys, young Spartans . . ."—Thom Gunn

•

like large projectiles & fruit of the sea

like interconnected oceans & oysters on the half shell

like what remained of the church

like children tasting alcohol for the first time [franz's formulation]

like merry gibbons & decals on the wrong car

like red riding hood crying on the bus

like sitting on a thumb & friends drifting apart

like a thermometer's mercury heart

like state troopers finding the llama

like stale chips & rancid salsa

like feeding johnny his lines [he forget]

like egg salad on challah

like *i didn't leave the republican party, the republican party left me*

like groping around for k-pop strays

like small *hi* & shit on ur lip

like *a little less conversation, a little more touch my body*

like sunburnt cheeks & long hours doing

like thoughts belonging to me & u

like silkworms which is weird since they are worms [!!!]

there is much to investigate

BEHIND THE COUNTER IN A SMALL TOWN

ralph the tortoise died, falling
& when it was the collector's turn, we went thru his stuff
raiding his place like locusts, a silence between us
he was, shall we say, a lifelong bachelor—
we expected some gems, figured we'd find hazy polaroids
albums of tricks cursed with restless beauty
how far into the season before the hate-crime episode ???
one image has proven inescapable—
boys in white shirts & khaki shorts
pushing a massive medicine ball
athletic socks pulled up, faces bewildered & pliant
here, resisting the easy analogy of sisyphus
& what a peculiar strength looks like
vaguely masochistic, this zest for life !!!
how ppl used to call bush "shrub"
to me, a cuter variant
hong kong's leader deemed "689"
not the margin, but votes received
in a rigged election
hi or lo, would u like to be a number
in my body count
see how one casual remark
can render the sum total of ur feelings
a nullity
still, i would rather be a lamppost in new york
than the mayor of philadelphia
i'd be ur seeing-eye dog
where it's never sunny
untangling the dense knot of love's invention
or intention
hard to tell, exactly
there's a quality of prescience i like in u
pinched bottlecap, improvised passion
& 3a train to pound town, obviously a tourist
making eyes, lifting his shirt,
slyly upturning the corners of his mouth
till his gf violently jerks his hand
the way u would yank a leash
if u were inconsiderate

or michael vick
erasing every poem that has claimed
he was “part horse” or red-winged demon
i suppose it doesn’t hurt to be cautiously optimistic—there—
long languid strokes

OPEN SESAME

love is everything it's said to be
pure as poison
i sat w/ prostitutes & lepers & u
a century's worth of grime
on this old master
in jabba's fantasy
leia as humiliated slave
they killed the clam bake
have rice for breakfast b/c they r azn
in erykah's formulation
they either want to be u
or have sex w/ u
somehow u satisfy both
i feel the words starting to move
" i'm a trained intimacy coach "
his disguise a movie
i accidentally saw twice
pardon my hungry eyes
open for u like a toaster
i think i'm all right

A CATHOLIC EDUCATION

the flowers were ready but the nuns refused to stand
fungal infections in the toe
spread across the convent
out of an abundance of caution
alarmed administrators canceled their trip to the city center
if nothing else
let this be the crotch u remember
i let poets lie to me
if they speak in complete sentences
raised limbs & *come here*
perfect arms perfect wingspan
he has interesting rules, takes my hand in his
i'm of the undisciplined variety
stolen love interest
still life w/ stranger
good men don't feel their husbands
or fear unlimited soup & salad
these flamin' hot cheetos proving useful
when i was confined to a suitcase
w/ an exceptional goat
the craft exploded
its occupants cooked like a burger
the titular cauboi put down the prime ortolan
& bloody napkin
one droplet to change ur life
we knew that he hoofed her
but weren't aware she was married
since i've never been to bhutan
during the war
i was an artist
painting animals w/ different-colored ears [red fox, black boar]
we hear ur complaints
know abt strolls in venice
love letters are always ambitious
not to put too fine a point on it
we don't call them shrimp in australia [that's a prawn]
woven strips of bread mimic curly tresses
like twisted horns
the annuals & perennials amused us

i'd like to talk abt the pie
now that nature includes a slice
how can we get our hands on it
a big slice tho we are not greedy
sometimes, he says, suddenly serious
u americans cut off ur nose to spite ur face

执迷不悔 UNREPENTANT

"What can I do but shine / in memory"—John Wieners

•

racing down a beach may reap uncommon rewards
a simple gift, one a ghost could give
when all's said & done, what have we got left
ghost nuts, a whole wad
[something to share]
ur breath on my chest
AG standing for "aspiring governor"
u will surely hate growing old
the constant yelping in the yard
followed by extended periods of pain
my mood depending upon the fireworks
i derive no pleasure from fantasies
indecent lips, carnal skin
unwholesome, vulgar
buggers to be awoken
ppl who disappear into side streets w/o warning
& never look back
on a day like today
remind me how the sunroom filled w/ ferns
over our protestations
the trip to echo park being unnecessary
it was the first good party of the season [some say the only]
baubles & balls
snow that keeps melting
after u shake it off
three bees on a shield
shiny headgear lifted from a learned man
reciting the dimensions of a dream

DREAM IN TWO PARTS

1/

make sure ur clean

the only thing worse than getting shot in the street

is getting shot in the street

w. a dirty ass

2/

<u>wants:</u>

for me to say *sorry*

for u to say *don't be*

for one (both?) of us to say

sissy

SNOW WHITE / FINAL GIRLS

joe the plumber died
burt hummel ran for congress
i signed up for apple tv+
to see dave franco
tight neck & romantic eyes
in guncheck blazer
bushy brows & hair like october
u'd know wut i mean
if u were classy
tongue pink as eraser
aggressively asserting *i - am - a - muscle*
chirp ur siren darling
embrace the promise of slay
u glitter w/ stones
this is why ppl inevitably fall in luv
& off the wagon
MIKE CHANG FOREVER
edited to say
MAKE CHANGE FOREVER
—typical
all the mothers singing
pickled by birds
shredded into wild ginger
peasants burned in ice
the cold creeping thru a crack
the lost lunchables
delivered w/ spells & delusion
he grew up amidst paddy fields & enthusiastic
[strenuous?] petting
wait, don't tell me:
shallots in gin
dip ur card into my machine
bob, hold me under the surf
stars, feathers & tassel

THINK FAST

the elevator arrives but u forget why ur there

too many days saying *not this*

or [worse] hearing *not chu*

chelsea handler opens the door

screaming into the phone

I'M OLIVIA MUNN

I DON'T GIVE A FUCK ABT UR MESSAGE !!!

giggling uncontrollably

great hair, can't breathe

who can, under all that armor

chicken tenders

a prolific dater roasting their dates

murdering them wit words

tickling their prostate

ur not supposed to say " murder " anymore

ur killing it

ur slaying it, sir slay

timothée's crabs crawl a little

don't worry, it isn't cum

why would u let me think that ???

have u, by chance, ever seen cum ???

so far, berrigan’s cum

all gone, more or less

it doesn’t get any realer than this

YOU'RE LIVING ALL OVER ME

in the city u rarely see pigeons dying of natural causes
it's fascinating where animals go to die
they w/ their keen sense of honing
say goodbye to chafing
he'll be remembered for once taking an epic holiday
& being felt up under his ribs
horseface sticking out over a gate
his scowling snail teeth
the hardest biological material
biting down on flaky wife cakes
chewy wintermelon filling
a natural womyn shipped canada post
maybe things would be better
if i woke & saw u
dressing gud & looking hot
imagine if the aliens came
& u were the first person they met
making contact w/ a mortal like u
thinking every human looked the same
tall as sequoia or redwood
hair color changing w/ the light
it'd be like if babe ruth were the first ballplayer
or jackson pollock the only septuagenarian
they'd ever met
don't u think it would blow their minds
every creature on the planet
tasting like chicken
warily eyeing the invalids at the table
u try different voices
choirboy scream *i wanna know where i came from !!!*
r u wut they call an earth angel
creeley didn't seem to understand that " sd " is *sugar daddy*
the probe was not painful
when we made love
roving over the expanse of ur cadaver-body
like roomba or space cruiser
[depending on budget]
pouring myself into u
prodigiously wet

an intense feeling like breaching a hideaway
notice how windy it gets down by the park
now i know this man never worked a day in his life

GROW UP & BLOW AWAY

I GIVE YOU TUG, TULIPS!

GRANT YOU DINOSAURS, RAMI MALEK'S TWIN!

THEY ARE 5-FOOT-4, TOTALLY SHREDDED!

PLOWED BY POET, SHOCK IN MY HANDS!

EAT MY TOFU, SLAP THAT CHILEAN BASS!

MICROAGGRESSION, LEAVE MONICA OUT OF THIS!

THE MAYOR GAVE THESE HORSES JOBS!

MADE YOU A CROSS-EYED BITCH!

TRIAL NOTES

boy running hand thru hair   the handsomest   slipping past

a miner's lungs   punched thru a window   feeling great

i too have done things for my luxury watch collection   born sad   may not even finish

i don't have any excuses   skedaddle outta here   señor fluffy

john's ashbery   pushing deftly thru me   blue lights discouraging jumpers

soft necks broken in low vases   destroying rotary phone   debunking race science

dream journal of nixon   tarot deck of virgin   imogen heap playing

mouth

RES JUDICATA

the thinker who claimed it was easy to be avant-garde
but hard to tell a simple story
was not smart enough to escape the lightning strike
or avoid the burning bush
we know he died in 1640
but when was he born
a loser
backbencher w. no charisma
best known as a visitor i fiddled w.
muttering incessantly abt leopard sharks
& other made-up creatures
when we broke up
ur dentist called indelicately
to say u missed ur appt
i combined my favorite activities
licking stars & sleeping thru it
all politics being local
ignoring my bruised foot
a fearful future
its semantics
splitting hairs for this high
pack of boys known as an allegation
substantiated like walking into woods
drunk but not disorderly
emerging w. phlox
& newfound knowledge
handpicked for u
a ramekin of warm nuts
followed by silence
will this pain ever stop

TOY SOLDIERS

our affections

build a ship in a basement

before figuring how to get it up

the stairs

*

u came from the same demonic womb

i washed the sexless lord outta my hair

left the blue imp in amsterdam

burping nasty back into a can

it was a different time

then

ANATOMY OF AN EVENING DIPTYCH

"After I fuck you, let me cry on your shoulder"—Future

•

to be taken to the cleaners   an auspicious event   only if it's the chinese laundry

owner dozing off w. radio on   i cut / u deal   everybody gets something

the same card in the same hand   one thing on top of another   we understand when to trade

how to play   w. my face on the floor   if u want to make god laugh   tell them ur a poet

haunting us like happiness

•

u moaning into a pillow abt needing more time, me leaning on u like a hospice cot, naked

knees, unclean hands, old new york post neatly folded, i beg— u pretend to sleep— a great

bloodlust shared between us like breath or an admission of love

BAD AT MATH

sitting here in my nightgown

greedy ppl living between places

bartender a boy named silver

who i imagine was properly put on trial

counterculture sagging from weight of my gravitas

i was flooded wit fuck jelly

it is v sad wut has happened to the drug trade

i read that time passes for animals differently

but really thinking of me & my nailbeds

when i'm not wit u

as i understand it

not liking wut the world has become

a rock & a hard place

won't stop talking abt fassbinder

the year versace was killed

as exclusive drug mule to phil collins

drinking my baby to death

by now issey miyake is also dead

u must be pressing ur cock into soft tits

as i recall it

i feel as if i have ruined my life

i wanna smuggle u into me

inside of me extremely ripe

will even go downtown for ur wet lips

those r the ways of the weasel

i wanna party in ur red eyes

young & in luv

this is the way i remember

REGIONAL ALL-STAR

ur outta my mind   the moment u lose ur erection
          reading   w. bastardization in ur voice
                                        my work-in-progress
working girl
w. client   inbred gettys
                                                  murderous pelosis
          if u treat ppl right the first time
                              u never have to apologize
                                        or hide the body
w. that   maurice ass name
                    wut century is he from   anyway
          i only have cute friends
                                        a guest editor who's a dugong
maybe he wants to snatch things off shelves w. u
                    have u tried asking in german
                                                  i tried playing w. u & u broke
my friend jason   (not the korean)   sez
          rocks are fucking gey
                              all rocks are fucking gey
                    & the merman's glittery prick   tastes horrible
          somebody throw a net on that   sea lettuce
something warm   to dip ur tongue in

2 HARD 2 LUV 2 YOUNG 2 DIE

1.] NUMB FUGGO STRANGER W. PRISTINE RECTUM

2.] MIND'S NARRATIVE UNKNOWABLE

3.] HAVE FEELINGS, MAKE BOOK, LIFE GREAT

4.] URS THE ONLY WORDS I NEED, I THINK I FEEL IT NOW, JUST LIKE U

5.] NOBODY READS POETRY, I REALLY SHOULDN'T ANYMORE

6.] SKIP AHEAD, LOOK WEAK, A BEATING WOULD DO US A LOT OF GUD

7.] WHITE FLAGS, Xs ON DOORS, FACES TWISTED W. DESIRE

8.] CEASE STRIVING, I'M SICK FOR U, DON'T U WANNA PET ME

9.] WANNA BE TIED TO BACK OF UR JEEP LIKE CAB DRIVER OR U.S. SENATOR

10.] WHAT DID J— SAY ABT FILLING U LIKE A CANOE, I DON'T REMEMBER

11.] IDENTIFYING CAUSE OF MY TREMBLE, R U READY TO SHOW ME SOME ASS

*.] DEVASTATING, INDESCRIBABLE, HOW WILL U TELL ME WHEN UR READY

广岛之恋 HIROSHIMA MON AMOUR

eyes flashing w. desire

my brother's friend

looks around for a mirror

sporting a familiar grin

can't countenance light

this shredded syntax

voice smooth as buttered noodle

rakes his haircut w. fingers

brain crowded w. boys

i rebel in lace & tulle

anything moving across it

a perfect blur

FUTURE PIRATE RADIO

fake rat blood trophy
joyce carol invented bigotry
the police have airpods in
bitch don't trust them
to burp me
eric i invented ur tush
w. the squarish indents
my fragile disposition
deserving of several oscars
she's not like the other goirls
she built different
than the goirls
crippling
yo bitch
not the first to leave
looking like little foot
high heel shu
hot chip n lies
our love is comprehensive
both sides of the tracks
vertebrate n invertebrate
single eyelid n double
black n pink
stonewall n clubs
thrown at cars
we tortured we genius
we slay we slain
we man we g.o.a.t.
pan's labyrinth
i'm iconic
she's a writer
gud luck to her
collapsed like cardboard
u wanna smash
wouldn't u like to
find out

SWEETHEART

clean ur front
lay down a towel
this ham sandwich is free

in the dark these ashtrays wink
that tower sizzles
deceived by the appearances of things

the bloodthirst of millennia
who can say which u prefer
it's ok to be dishonest

the buss takes me
like hog to slaughter
say how u want me

nothing beats whiteboys in red shorts
flattened by a vending machine
more lifeless each year

u sit on the fire escape
life's most enduring questions
between moments in the sun

not ok to be tedious
get off my back bernadette
i don't take the buss

solid not standout
i have no teachers
we take them for a ride

SATURDAY NIGHT

I think abt how dinner service was not disrupted
when I undid ur jeans w. the zeal of a colonizer
This kinky role-reversal
& lovely roleplay
which u thought was only possible w. true love
How u looked at me like a malnourished calf eyeing a bottle
How I pulled & pulled & pulled on u like a Czech
I think that's ok to say
My feeling an irresponsible amount of fondness
equal to the time I was deflowered by Sharon's very large Boy
the one who owned everything, including my proud bresses
How I am the only one who knows him —still

ROSE & CUIR

actually i don't think i'd mind

u knowing my sweat & sperm

like obscure lyrics committed to memory

or a cascading fountain after the fall of gaddafi

i realize it's customary to say i'm *giving in* to night

but sleep i'm not the surrendering kind

take me evening w. honeyed limbs

i like how u sometimes come apart

neither cheap nor a thrill sorta unhinged

everything sluggish complications a consensus choice

suppose we ignore things that aren't me

roll our eyes at grief & prizes for poets over 40

i read these poems & think u will fuck these poets

fuck the shit outta them yes we know the truth

just do it fuck their buckteeth straight

liz claiborne headbands all bent outta shape

dispose of them & remind them ur a fuccboi

ur mastercock hopping a chainlink fence

leaving them alone w. their garbage snoozer poems

shivering colors & small towns in italics

come back to me give me ur stomach

press into me allow me one small happiness

BLUE TINT

"I blame it on Blake, on Robert Aldrich's Kiss Me, Deadly"—O'Hara

•

white lady complimenting my houndstooth coat

shamelessly comparing it to her mother's

i pull my coat closer

tell her *i am ur mother !!!*

lecture her on voting rights

how never to put "rat-a-tat-tat" in a poem

u start flinging pearls at her

no great loss for swine

ur riding too high to care

we build a fence to keep out bad poets

opinions on every robocop remake

i find a scrum of rugby players eager to fill u

w. knowledge

the thinnest-skinned man on park ave

stretching out the crotch of teal lingerie

a hussy ordered online

distracted by the hiss of subway

thinking it was seafoam

IN SPITE OF OURSELVES

save ur affection for me   scouts rubbing sticks   i hate ur abundance   fall to pieces

_ust thinking abt it   just thinking abt it   can get me in trouble

tho my tits appear calm   this heaven's big enough for 2

like sword returning to scabbard   rolling dung in elephant enclosure

a broken clock is right twice a day

SO SAD (TO SEE GOOD LOVE GO BAD)

I Can't

Come Over

To-Nite

I Don't

Know Who

You Are

Great

Big

Penis

Heavy

Lidded

Eyes

I Don't

Want To

Force You

I Won't

Be Able

To Stay

Who Are

We To

Dream So Loud

1 A.M. PLAYDATE WITH CHEMISTRY SET

did u cast a ballot for whiteboys, their nutrition

so tall & made of cream

the boys go at each other w. bats

in some misguided, macho episode

w. unfathomable, unbelievable results

for the other members of the regional team

having gone to law school before roe died, still living that reality

impressive dissertation, first prize & free dessert

thank u for asking

every arsonist every bombmaker

has a signature

most liars

have a tell

adam screaming mighty innards at serpent

57TH STREET DIPTYCH

I

oh i saw olga too tho not the olga i was expecting *jesus fucking christ ogre* how many ogres can there be tomorrow when it's nothing but short knights w. long lances yearly calendars for 2022 b/c u represent the past i can't stop thinking abt how my friend who lived near the flatiron had a urinal installed b/c he refused to pee sitting down righting wrongs the right plugs in the wrong sockets shock the system like a paper plane loose & free lord of the flies hating how they don't have a/c in all of europe ""those ppl"" on strike for the right not to refrigerate their butter a radical course of action can't compete don't compare the only person too modest to get what they want in-between sips forget it forget it so hard crying like smart person billy magnussen stumbling not drunk patch of grass

II

watch as i saunter along not drunk imagining a long line of txt serving as a cap for even more txt below like a proud graduate of animal husbandry or jay sebring the magical hairdresser a jilted lover who is one fateful evening hopelessly (helplessly?) murdered reminding me of my model cum hairstylist james who has the exact same birthday as me down to the year he turns 30 upon which he is promptly typecast as pretty & confused young dad or mfa student w. behavioral issues accused of writing for the white geys / gaze i could never figure out which which i suppose is a better outcome than not going quietly whilst viciously chowing down on something w. webbed feet as they say a *pato*

都会感 METROPOLITAN FEELS

w/ now-deleted posts

amy schumer accused of cyberbullying nicole kidman

he loved me but lived too far !!!

u otherworldly u ethereal creature from diff plane

for u i'm gasping guppy

for u i'll do the mouth thing help get u off no recip necessary

two nasty dolls truly deviant pouches of warmth

we trust we verify this muzzle

pressed to skin texture of toast

i'll tell her the bus is here

u see we never put our eggs in one basket

shriveled dried up plums in any stocking

halston's bloodline dying out

swiftboated kerry u paw u pay

amber heard's doctor the full measure of cock

hair soft sweetly scented ugly gurls be quiet

u dislodge him from muse-throne

blame his baby peccary his maialino

only a sick cashew like u

could accomplish such a feat

nobel for loneliness

breathless in wonderment

fresh tears dashing from eyes

proud to say that child is gay !!!

HEY HIGHROLLER

i'm in a remote cabin in the cascades
my printer's down
the frogs can't swallow w/ their eyes open

could u tell me the difference between
an optician & an optometrist
i lost u in the clouds

how was carmen electra's first & only album
on prince's paisley park label
it is self-titled

do u speak ur peace
can i hold ur piece
jewels knocking me over like a swinging gate

the city's full of murderers & maniacs
plus whatever peanut butters ur jelly
who else can call me brave

who else can teach me

I WANNA BE WRONG

wanna sleep till i see u again
words u generally wanna hear
except when ur already at their haus
hey do u wanna get outta here
i like it when u talk abt cannes
so much
i like it so much
i'm a same-sex couple
a warehouse
nothing in me but a grand piano
stop staring
start tearing
if u'd changed u wouldn't be here
did u see my present
the one i left
believing u could be deterred
i think i threw it out
as they used to say in hollywood
that movie sold popcorn
he asked to take me to the pound shop
but it was just a dollar tree
u go to the disco, panic
they want a better look at u
any acknowledgment of their infinitesimal existence
as mark twain's old saw has it
the difference between a fire & a firefly
rain that looks like u, clean sheets
we luv to be intrusive
take an invasive procedure
make it more invasive
find it hard to leave relationships
luv being in luv w/ machines
money from a white-shoe firm
in fact a frozen-foods conglomerate
angel cakes bearing lines of credit
do not be afraid

THIS HELL IS BETTER WITH YOU

Pls don't tell Eric

Abt the flesh-eating bacteria in the lake

Where he has gone swimming

He went to Michigan

& knows a love that only grows thicker & heavier

Like an athlete's corded neck

His powerfully-naked back at Berlusconi's bunga bunga

How's that for feminism

Camped out somewhere in Big Sur

Jessie's girl deep inside me

My face open for overanalysis

Pendleton blankets on vivid display

The thump of falling apples

Impressive size of bear

The ants going to town

An accepting kind of community

This packet of bolognese much too sweet

A lot—too much—riding on ur acquiescence

SPECIAL SNOOZE

When u tell me abt ur experience on the train
w/ the Congressional "helper"

I start to laugh
partly b/c the correct term is *staffer*

partly b/c I don't want to admit that I am happy
in case it gets taken away from me

—this happiness emanating from our general vicinity
So I shut my mouth, careful not to show teeth

The same way I suppose tribes of animals
tend to be mindful of when they bare their fangs

if the gods are watching
I'm not allowed to be too happy

I'm not sure why I think this
Probably something learned from television

specifically The Mentalist on CBS
where I noticed that Harry Styles has the exact same face

as River Phoenix
All I know is:

There will be hell to pay
for our reckless disregard

not necessarily for the truth
But for our shared circumstances

MIND YOUR OWN BIZNIT

an eel & a conger like u very much
or each other
they like each other very much
how ur DNA may be 99.9% similar
but u absolutely don't care
how it feels to be ashamed of a child
& will never live up to ur mother's example
with those dogshit poems
cursing u from her grave or the next room
she doesn't have much time left
before her date picks her up
& not being long for this world
the eels r ready for a frenzy
they say u want a new boi in u
looking before doing
like a mysterious cat
u confirm:
only to possess
& seem excited by the prospect
like a cancer that comes back
my door is always open
but never for that

IN THE FIELD WHERE I FOUND US

slipping tongues in mouth-slots

i'm a barbarian

hunting ur perfect limbs

ur ideal flesh

tickling ur immaculate ivories

ur throat feeling plummy

i enjoy it reluctantly

just kidding

i like it so hard it loses all meaning

we come from disparate corners

u sit mad & jealous

stretched out on scratchy flannel

by the UN

where the trees are taller

the air is clearer

we share breath

climate is on the agenda

i know it by heart

look at us:

so smug & satisfied

two whites in safari hats

magicians lifting cloches

bunnies smoothing over cowlicks

least painful elegy already written

MEET ME HALFWAY , AT LEAST

internet socialist u do too much trying to sell

[dance-jam escapism as revolution]

thin skin glass jaw tell me what i'm missing

[sinners , curdled anger , david foster wallace]

cultural vandalism half-baked knock-offs generic sloganeering

[obligatory song abt being on the road]

before he cheats hot girl bummer white boy summer

[squeezed , shaped , unfounded suspicion]

so hot it hurt my feelings i wanna turn into u desire

[missing someone , irrationally]

like when u sleep thimble-full of discreet majesty so unawares

[the wings keeping ur heart in the clouds]

get busy living get busy dying the reason these tables are numbered

[the anchor keeping my feet to the ground]

do ur part stop going to shows save the scene looking straight at me

[the lights deceiving even the rice ppl , hunny]

those that know know all too well how bad licorice can taste

[laid out in the sun , sorry , meaning u]

i will never write too much suckerpunch

[reward , relief , u will think it yet]

SELVEDGE DENIM

No resisting what has shaped me:
several years ago
I signed up for an email list
that paid off enormously

They started to drop like flies:
Walt's spectacular swimmer
A solitary giant
hasty to delight in my maidenhead

My flabby length
& Phil Collins's daughter
in a carriage drawn by sleek otters

We don't feel the need to hide from prying eyes
or show restraint
in the face of godlike bodies

How fortune favors ignoramuses immense & real
The most confident of whom are
" fiscally conservative & socially liberal "

Hips rocking softly
Liquid lips sloshing distractedly

I get agitated licking their shitter
In me a nauseating mistrust akin to seasickness

The build & promise of a breakthru

At last a shriek

UNDER MILK WOOD

as in glass onion

where the genius turns out to be an idiot

doofy asks asinine questions

writes uninspired, off-putting

white-savior essays

doofy, don't gamble wit my career

come talk to me when u have

this gorgeous housing

i wish i could ignore ur wide nasal wings

& white flesh like pomfret

just drop ur twee poem in the ocean

sidestep the bodies in dirty denim

watch me sit here

dreaming of cups that fill themselves

wit ghee fat

the celibate thom / tim gunn

a peculiar perfume

i've been so patiently

waiting for

yes, i think he's easy to adore

like the length of a car

—too much to take

BREATHE UNDERWATER

The dog has sneezed.

I am chaste.

The sword in the stone.

I'm in my Empress energy.

The archers are lining up.

You are a pussy magnet.

You use me for content.

Hollow sidewalk will not support vehicles.

I have nothing important to communicate.

You have suffered a great disappointment.

Maybe the trouble is you're good at the world of things, words.

But love is not something ~~you~~ one can ever be good at.

I don't know how to square that circle.

Only a poet does.

I never remember the shit he says because he's never had an original thought.

Or said anything worth repeating.

He eats 12 eggs for breakfast.

Says such things as *I don't know why people choose to be poor.*

It's not a problem if money can fix it.

He really spreads his seed.

I'm keeping my nose clean.

I want to prove the world wrong.

I'm waiting for the other shoe to drop.

愁 SORROW

obzezzed w. ur black nylon
shorts, we hate wut we have
released like the tide
            something to run after

sent to the closet, never
to emerge (the ultimate
compliment)
i am where a weed can grow
            don't turn ur back on me

2 assistants, lotsa lunches
brainpower expended on
needy young butchers
            my peers have no respect

the harbormaster's prom,
recorded in ur lil ledger
wuz a prom   (half a promise)
            friendship is on the decline

teasing shards, twin beds pushed together,
things r not wut they seem
poetry cataloging societal ills
            the error of ur ways

resist the urge, deign an
apology, we've seen better
days
if ur not an aircraft   why r u
            announcing ur departure

one last thing, wild boy
w. penis envy
take wut u can fit in ur pockets
            take it all

NEPO BABY

. . . mishearing what language is in the body

for what *languishes* in the body . . .

i charge towards u . . .

my brother's keeper . . .

could the difference between us be any larger than . . .

john lewis, civil rights hero (here) . . .

john lewis, high-end department store (in england) . . .

tell everyone . . .

the only honest thing u've ever thought . . .

watch as they gather a loving mouthful of breast . . .

peer out from behind those *exquisite* bangs . . .

absolutely certain every song was abt u . . .

the rest of us looking down at red solo cups . . .

hoping we could be somewhere else, anywhere else . . .

wondering who had misspoken . . .

& what exactly happened here

NEW NATIONAL ANTHEM

when i awoke in that hotel room

meg ryan was unrecognizable

u were sucking on my toes

the boy w. soft leg hair & contour butt

was no longer the frontrunner

for student council president

in a manner of speaking he was making moves

the way a dump truck backs up

she faked her birthdate to get in the club

only to change it again

to stay on her mom's insurance

pointing to her wounds

after i eviscerated her outfit & dye job

i did not offer comment on the obit

despite a long backlog of lines from yogi berra

the jock w. the fiery farts misquoting me

was stabbed selling counterfeit basquiats

& later killed by friendly fire

but not before thoroughly examining my insides

like a brute outside city lights

he showed me his poems

which were actually quite good

mostly concerning blake’s flap of boxer

i had no idea they knew each other

GLORIOUS GAME

"I think within his parameters / Clarence went the distance"—Ai

•

There are many problems with the Supreme Court today, not that we've noticed or cared enough to notice. We've lost the ability to be shocked and awed. Nonplussed about the private lives of politicians (how very French of us), our tolerance for the most ridiculous, illegal, immoral acts has increased. Tested with breaking news and ~critical~ ~information~ everyday, few things ragnarok us. A frat boy come super-senior year, we find ourselves groggier, paunchier, and somehow less in touch with the people around us than when we started this whole shebang.

From Clarence Thomas's well-publicized gifts scandal to his wife's nefarious comingling of private and public business (not to mention her insidious involvement in the January 6 coup attempt), the public has lost its appetite for Supreme Court scandal. And that's only one Justice !!! Like hearing your parents have sex, we endeavor to know as little as possible and to forget it even sooner.

Former New Hampshire Attorney General Michael Delaney's nomination to the Court of Appeals for the First Circuit was pulled because some Senators were displeased with the way he handled an abuse case involving a local private school. Even the once ironclad notion that lawyers should not be punished for who they choose to represent, a foundational principle that everyone deserves representation blah blah blah, has been challenged by Trump, Giuliani, and assorted shitstains.

But the threatened norm du jour is the bedrock principle of comity and collegiality on the Court. It wasn't that long ago that tales of Scalia and RBG going to the opera together breathlessly spread through town, look how they can come down on different sides of thorny legal issues, nay, the biggest issues in the land, and still remain such good friends—the kind of backslapping good ol' boy, nothing matters so long as I can make my tee time, nonsense I was brought up to hate. What these clueless observers don't know is this: the Justices got along swimmingly because THEY DON'T CARE ABOUT YOU. The cardinal sin of poetry (no stakes) has been a pattern and practice of legal systems since time immemorial, and judges have not been immune.

I'd noticed a steady erosion of haw-haw-haw good humor amongst the Justices and wondered if the Justices' *clerks* had gotten more partisan and rancorous (I would know, having clerked for two federal judges). My interest was additionally piqued by a case before the Court, *Andy Warhol Foundation for Visual Arts v. Goldsmith*, because my friend Robbie worked for Andy at Interview magazine and also because of a little tit-for-tat Justices Sotomayor and Kagan (incidentally both unmarried New Yorkers, as the tabloids often remind us) had going on in dueling opinions.

To make things simple: the Court ruled in favor of Lynn Goldsmith, a photographer who took a picture of Prince in the early 80s that Andy turned into colored silkscreens. The Warhol Foundation argued that the works were transformative and fair-use, but the majority reasoned that taking another artist's image and then licensing the new version for commercial use weighs against the fair-use defense.

By the numbers this was not a controversial case, decided 7-2, in an opinion authored by Sotomayor. Gorsuch filed a concurrence, which Jackson joined; Kagan dissented along with the Chief Justice. (It is probably important context that Sotomayor is seen by many as one of the Court's weakest writers, while Kagan is seen as the strongest post-Scalia.) Kagan quickly disses Sotomayor (well, technically the majority opinion), saying:

One preliminary note before beginning in earnest. As readers are by now aware, the majority opinion is trained on this dissent in a way majority opinions seldom are. Maybe that makes the majority opinion self-refuting? After all, a dissent with "no theory" and "[n]o reason" is not one usually thought to merit pages of commentary and fistfuls of comeback footnotes ... In any event, I'll not attempt to rebut point for point the majority's varied accusations; instead, I'll mainly rest on my original submission. I'll just make two suggestions about reading what follows. First, when you see that my description of a precedent differs from the majority's, go take a look at the decision. Second, when you come across an argument that you recall the majority took issue with, go back to its response and ask yourself about the ratio of reasoning to ipse dixit. With these two recommendations, I'll take my chances on readers' good judgment.

Dear reader, do you need first aid, because that's a burn !!!

As much as I enjoy Kagan's snark, part of what she's saying is bizarre: it's the rice pudding scream-asking the pot roast "why you so obsessed with me ???" when everybody knows the pot roast is the main attraction, the star of the show.

When I saw the rest of what she says though, I collapsed like the buildings at the end of Inception, I believe that's what occurs, I've never actually seen Inception. Kagan essentially calls out Sotomayor and the majority for twisting, recasting, mischaracterizing precedent—something, gasp, only conservatives do (admittedly to great result for their side, a nightmare for the rest of us, see recent North Carolina gerrymander case, for example). Kagan also says that Sotomayor's legal reasoning is weak sauce, it has no seasoning, take a seat, come back when you're ready to play in the big leagues.

To confuse matters further, Sotomayor admittedly does cite the dissent some 40-odd times. The majority opinion states, albeit with slight drunk shakes:

The dissent begins with a sleight of hand, and continues with a false equivalence between AWF's commercial licensing and Warhol's original creation. The result is a series of misstatements and exaggerations, from the dissent's very first sentence ("Today, the Court declares that Andy Warhol's eye-popping silkscreen of Prince ... is (in copyright lingo) not 'transformative'"), to its very last ("[The majority opinion] will make our world poorer").

What a muddying of the waters !!!

In the majority's view, copyright law's first fair-use factor—addressing "the purpose and character" of "the use made of a work"—is uninterested in the distinctiveness and newness of Warhol's piece. What instead matters under that factor is that Warhol's licensing of the silkscreen to a magazine precludes fair use.

So where do we stand on this—do we hurrah Warhol's obvious artistic magnificence and impact or do we in fact pay the artist (in this case photographer) ??? The law makes things so difficult !!!

Perhaps, as with most matters of the heart, the simplest explanation holds the answer.

"*I have this thing where I get older but just never wiser*"—ah, yes, it always comes back to Taylor.

SAVING THE WORLD

how is it that i've lived this long & nobody's ever said: *i should put a bell on u* ???
countless bell ends yet no bells
is it my quiet bound feet
[another wish: to be quietly bound]
don't tamp down my AZN JOY
my heart rate slowed but the tox screen was inconclusive
keep this talent liaison away from the celebrity wives—he is dangerous !!!
why, why did u choose this one
looking like roadkill
grief brought us together—i gave the order to shoot her
it's unforgivable what she has done
for dasani in the prisons & public schools
he was run off campus after being hazed by chiang kai-shek's great-niece
it wasn't a book review but a puff piece abt kitty litter
i enjoy my new poems
they feel like me but also not-me, in a good way
[that's something artists say to sound important]
there u are, useless as a curling iron in the wrong voltage
it's just something that gets easier as u go, fish on a bicycle
did u think that was too degenerate, dwarves at the spanish court ???
in the 18th century noblewomen wore monkeys
on the shoulder to make themselves look more beautiful
in contrast, six weeks ago i was on a rooftop w/ a champagne heir
fighting off a deranged bulgarian weightlifter
now my lover is a movie star, stubborn as a bunion, he's casanova
coming home w/ an armful of worthless prints, he just gave his last interview
under the pretext of getting comfortable, he edged his lips closer & closer to mine
i eyed the platter of breadsticks, individually-wrapped in prosciutto
a miserable snack, very proletariat
unbecoming of a man whose grandfather created babar the elephant
my country hasn't been around that long & ur already two-timing her
poetry aims at difficult meanings but i don't think ALL poetry is political
[the ppl who say that just don't have range]

my poetry is aimed at destroying ugly shit
i have it on good authority that white men w/ yellowed soles piss in
the shower
a design flaw, perhaps
he went to rehab to dodge charges but came out w/ a sex addiction &
fondness for the sopranos
old dirty bastid propelled by romance, passion for the youth vote
enviable
i ran to face the streets alone, these jellied candies meant to be
admired
never eaten or fed piece-by-piece w/ antique tongs
when he pulled me into bed
of coz i was wrong abt that, too
i mean falling asleep next to u
white linen shirt so flattering
not like my father's
nope, not at all

TASMANIAN DEVIL

u disloyal bitch
i am ur widow
ur princess in a tower
lazy pet chicken or fish [both]
fiction is easy to sell to twats
gloomy over ur poor loving
phantom lovers breed
violent blossoms
my favorite memory of u
is every memory
she doesn't know i hate her b/c
she looks like somebody
u would've fucked
& she is a kissinger
impossible testicle face all screwy
ras baraka devoured a royale w/ cheese
he works at the amiri baraka regional hospital
i can tell u abt him
but first let's discuss u
prowler of hearts
ur overgrown sex set off the alarms
the officers moved in when the dogs alerted
here we are
shameless graverobbers
the frat boy fixing his collar—adjusting himself—
touching the bell

POEM, DESCRIPTIVE OF RURAL LIFE & SCENERY (INCOMPLETE)

. . . has anyone ever broken down a door & found happiness on the other side throat magic & recouped time spent waiting for one goldberg or another reeking of cheap aftershave some YMCA brand the vendor unlicensed the first gentleman entering a swamp in search of his mate it was majestic it was maddening it was a pleasant evening at the london drugs the horse carcasses not too far away the beefcake in the pale shorts of a material so sheer as to be translucent two perfect globes of peach peeking thru before he sidesteps & reveals nay puts into view an equally blond colossus they might as well be twins skin bounce so sexy splendid honest jets of sperm sliding down thighs messy cackle driving dogs insane huge sections of town condemned landing gears engaged & our black hearts spared he did not apologize for he had the great fortune of being born w/ one temperamental as whiskey sky raining, well, carnivorous fish . . .

LAKE WALLENPAUPACK

go smoke a doobie norman dubie
u look pink as a poodle
we'll take cold lemonade & hot bodies intertwined
don't let her sink evil claws into u
like the scene in inglorious basterds
where the wrong hand gesture
gets everyone shot up
i know ur a slippery one
up in the crow's nest where ppl spend all day baking
high summer, arms sore
we can go anywhere
in a car
up urs sea-hunting
the joke ends w/ u a little hoarse
if ur lucky we'll take care of the last mile
it's a privilege: lobsters in the right pot & butter to be choked down
i don't trust fowl or a sibling rivalry
over the queer themes in evangelion
remember bail funds & all joy being valid
i'm similarly inclined to bite the biggest raccoon
he can run, but he can't hide, the sheriff said
abt the basketball player
built like a brick shithouse
joining hundreds of high-achievers for asparagus pee
the consulate texted an alert that the balcony was over capacity
we were intent on the view & imported parfum
u idiot they don't make fresca anymore !!!
i was late to my typing class
we insisted on being skullfucked
a pus-squirrel, impassive as grass
tiny heart crushed, useless
the case was closed w/o satisfactory resolution
i don't believe in ppl who dress poorly
so ignored bourdain's passing
keep thinking abt bidart stating
there was no place in nature where we could meet
barthes claiming " i miss u " always marking a concession
a surrendering of masculinity
& pollard howling *her breath smelled like straight-up shit*

—disclosures that feel untimely, unwelcome
i promise u couldn't be further away
forgotten like the gentle rolling of the hills
i haven't got the stomach for horseshit
this is a lake

LUMBER LIQUIDATOR

w/ u i only know the tip of the iceberg
& want to know more
it isn't fair that chief justice rehnquist
ordered mr conrad to live in a dumpster
behind the king of prussia mall
he's lost the plot, he can't be bothered
ms feinstein admitted to poisoning the chief
he killed earth during a drug-fuelled romp
his powerful ejaculate did not apologize
in an effort to cut costs
ms feinstein confessed to having written
all of these books
there r no longer bibles in every room
champagne available upon request
only the good brands, not that veuve shit
even tho (b/c?) he played a cop on teevee
they would not allow him near the meeting
in brooklyn everyone is smelly
& has read too much pynchon
particularly gravity's rainbow
which i imagine
must be part of some gay agenda
the boy hugged me in sondheim's house
like he meant it
presumably b/c there is love
they hired me to perform at some shindig
the rate they paid wouldn't even cover a decent lunch
or 5 martinis
it's criminal how they expect u to work
w/ fewer than 5 martinis in ur system
that balance beam being extremely sturdy
in a way it's sad what happened to robin's family
& brandon lee's issue w/ prop gun
tho i realize these things r not the same
since robin was taken in by a rich patron
becoming what we now consider well-kept
& brandon is dead
i hope u remembered * waterproof *
as tears will be shed

in an effort to keep me down
bonnie raitt said *never write abt love*
i've already surpassed her
i luv bonnie & her stretched mind
when i misread wonderment for " wondermeat "
i thought, yes, his meat is quite wonderful
tho i do not care for poodle
get ur pussy out the gutter
she cold

SOFT AS SNOW (BUT WARM INSIDE)

there's no nutrition in a muffin   patron saint of mixed messages
comes out of me chapter & verse   a troll-themed town
less room for error   what color helmet u want ???
he was never the same   after talking to chatGPT
which had somehow convinced him   that armani was secretly british
his suspicions seemingly confirmed   he went down the rabbit hole
an earthly hare   a brazen thief blowing thru intersections
body fit to the point of parody   the male whore spat *i am the (212) number*
working himself into a froth   beestung lips refusing to burst
sulky & pouty   inspiring mockery   " not quite there " as social lubricant
it must be vacca on the street   old cow   skunks ape
there isn't any reason   my love comes in different sizes
lead singer of a forgotten band   tells me to use my imagination
gargoyle in a gown   i am out of place
can only come up w. passion   rainbow beachball i turn over & over in my head
how u are a *nice boy—nice boy—nice boy*   or i was hearing my own suffering
cuz boys are mostly hair
i think abt how i must be a better poet than u   since u are dead
& i'll only keep getting better   wouldn't u agree
i find u compelling   the right shade of raspberry
like the one who said everything is impermanent   including his incredible body
tho i'm pretty sure he still loves me   the way u put ur hand on a stove

out of love or some misguided desire   i’m trying to convince myself
i don’t have a chosen family   but at some point i stop
        —i choose me

HEAVEN.ZIP

i recognized u by the swoosh on ur shus
& what for anyone else would constitute
clouds of musk
u are for me 命根子
my lifeblood
the root giving life
i want to chase, squabble over u
u are, shall we say, hen-pecked
meeting most overtures w/ such unvarnished cruelty
u have everybody's full attention
yet are torn between the ham-hock
& the big-breasted coquette
muses, i am not " led by the nose "
there is no leading
there is no nose
the beleaguered executive resigning in disgrace
became a den mother to a local sorority
[not one of the better houses]
& downed too much red wine
before operating heavy machinery
as the chief regina would later sheepishly admit
joke's on u, the apricot-plum & casablanca tagines
taste exactly the same
yes, this froth tells me
it's not the same ocean as before
i'm sorry ur kind is dying out
red hair is so nice
ur head looks like a raging fire
dusk touching unsullied roof
the sounds of an amateur musician
disappearing into evening
who am i to judge

BORN CALLOUS

when i say “ poem ”
u say
TRUMP DELIVERED JUSTICE IN CENTRAL PARK
we say
give us some clarity
they were crazy for each other
while refraining from long drives w. lesser kennedys
they were devoted to the conservative cause
& a small desert rat
which brought the syphilitic boy to tears
truthfully, it’s no longer politic to say
“ blind as a bat ”
the pornographer must first figure out
the root cause of his blindness
amidst a tenderness
i see all the things i did
everyone can see it
sick panic, i assure u
when sinéad o’connor said mc hammer made sexist remarks
& smelled like coconut
i knew not bizet nor vivaldi
invited john’s aromatherapy boys
to feel the loopty-loop of fraternity
weak !!! hands off my mongol beef !!!
when was the last time hillary did the dishes ???
house she learned to sleepwalk
by memorizing the floorplan
beating the game kobayashi maru
raúl the peacock screeched his displeasure
bleeding into the sheets
the elephant felt nothing for the three blind mice
do not devalue their myopic experience, by extension, cock
they did not choose to be born
bright-eyed & bushy-tailed germans
who would not shut up abt the gesamtkunstwerk
young, skinny, a fine tail on that donkey
stagehand w. studly glare & black air force ones
if u were to say *dick me down*
i would say *get in the van*

or *did u lose ur place in line*
乔治·克鲁尼
means george clooney
克鲁 克鲁
is cloo-cloo in mandarin
a cooing pigeon
digging this jam

MATCHMAKER

not simple, is it, for u to be vulnerable & free
to relish this love
look on imdb & see ur character's been killed off
i loved him in that general way
it's much too late for specifics
too indulgent like a hot skunk
erupted glans & sacs of stink
remind me of ur cologne
being purposefully undignified
he plants carrot seeds in belly button
what adrienne called *the dream-site*
tho she was talking abt new york
good news: i've finally enrolled u in swimming classes
bravo, nice fit, my god, so tight
she provided the correct prognosis, this profit-pig
grunted & yelped in porcine pleasure
as if pumped full of hormones
till u had visions, dimples on a schoolboy, such a rude delight
the french open a wooded area
miss ting my music teacher
wooed by lover who made fortune in palm oil
& attended to her deepest parts
accomplishing the impossible TUCK
how i adore dancing to the rhythm of those words
slick as palm oil
i cannot forget the sweetest of scenes
miss ting quaking when her mac made a noise
she blamed limerence, sang like a nightingale
" we'll see abt that !!! "
nice title for negligible thing
dispatch from jimmy: sea tumbled as sheets ???
yes, i think so
pome lifted from me
nary a feature in sight
not just for the fans
but the casuals, the glorious one
scheming his way into bosom of rich fairy
his holiness, the perennial problem child
in mobile-friendly coffin

look what u made me do
nobody plant roses
lost tapes stay lost
band keep playing
go at it
duck & drake
as one

THE LOVELIEST TIME

"In the afternoon they came unto a land / in which it seemed always afternoon"
—Alfred, Lord Tennyson

•

they r lazy
they slack off
grief looks different for everyone
estranged husband uninvited to sit up front w. family
horses on the battlefield, immovable, weeping
this business w. the dominos behind us
breakdown or breakthru: don't dare question me !!!
i know myself & have chosen another kind of attention
lasertag having gone the way of velcro
like ur career it's fallen by the wayside
he became speaker in a power-sharing deal
but hadn't been seen in public for a long time
shying away from events & living off the proceeds of a sale
when he unloaded his greek villa to the dutch king
(then the prince of orange)
passing the cancer-stick back & forth
he had the sudden realization
that if some heinous disease claimed his beloved
he'd sentence himself to an equally lamentable death
throwing himself off the tram
it suited him, that environment, the stakes not too high
keeping in mind that the shelves were never dry
photos of the falling men marked classified & put away
the great ox convinced he had reached the end
little did he know his life was just beginning
in these fair suburbs he was highly-favored
the lonely tigress had many role models & no discernible accent
in april she was named chairwoman of america first action
let me officially welcome u back into the fold
i think we were surprised by ur kindness & modest taste in wine
dumb conjecture
to be intent on a man
armed w. cheekbones that could cut glass
boys who smell nice or toss their hair

gestures that don't mean anything
incredible, immaculate, forgiveness forthcoming
it is no good to smoke
it was all a coming-on

GROUNDHOG DAY

when u get up & go
wagging ur eyebrows
my following after u
feels inexorable as fingers running thru jelly

dog-nails clacking on floorboards
postcards w. no return address
for a while i was hiding
admiring from afar

begging in private
studying u as my beacon
now i have nowhere to hide
but u

i know it isn't sensible
looking to u to fix my lack
or carry me thru the day
i just saw u

shared glint of recognition
i hope to see u again
illuminated numerals on a watch
i don't want to tell the time

can only recall these lines from lewis:
right now ur probably by the ocean
while i'm still out here in the rain
the same but not quite—

endearing in our inelegance
perfect in our incongruity
the birds in pictures
practicing their calls

ur sound
still here
its source
emitting all light

THE ORIGINAL WAS BETTER

wut did jasmine tookes took   lunch in fur   tight & hot   the hot pain of it
lapping at me   barrel-chested & somehow on his heels   anteater most zoo-like
ravenous man in impala   don't understand hats   why hide ur most important asset
arrogant italian youths   employees pushing rollercoaster   stuck on sister
jammed in the tracks   the one who survived murder-for-hire plot
tilda swinton's emails w/ margaret cho   abt whitewashing in hollywood
we've never met, but u've been in my head for years   did u say come let me touch u   [a terrible mistake]
can only luv between cat & tree   said to differ from the black mountain poets
executive doesn't feel bad abt firing worker   who saved his life on 9/11   " not a charity "
he returns to bed giddy   glazed w/ seamen on shore leave
seen book on dinners that changed the course of history
can't promise that but would like to spend time w/ u   this weekend   one labors like a mustang
wut r ur daily needs shallow hal   wut cliff wut criteria   house purportedly a lemon
eerie cry from shower   after long day's work   doing battle w/ emperor
when u met him he was a mutant   time rolls around   owls hoot farewell
cockroaches robbed & beaten   stagecoach driver striking back at tiresome friends
this tomahawk steak   cannot be called that   once u've said something   that's it
sponges r simple: load the gold   sail back to britain   the vampiric way they pop up
making a pass   *i say, i say*   in the mincing way of englishmen   gazing at the ganges
a little lost as if palming immense tackle   tiny wealthy boys   i hold to my lady opening
this old thing ???   worth a million dollars   thru layers of glass
impassive as a mannequin   which is   of coz   wut he was

浪漫杀死巨蟹座 ROMANCE KILLED THE KRABBY

why hate on his rolex
as if it were ripped from wrist of immigrant
his hetero predispositions / preoccupations
like sunglasses
u see what i see
courage the cowardly dog
don't call us, we'll call u
bark bark
bitter & nosy
doofy not appreciate when i make gey krabby
i explain u kamala sty
there is continent called n. america w. sexy krabby
i make him gey
work-in-progress like rama x ascension
diane had so much fudge
she could run a marathon
w. pekingese nipping at her heels
wandering abt the whitney
holding obligatory chunk of lapis lazuli
unironically mutter abt every single thing
i had a sex dream that began like this
or *i need to install one of these in my house*
fish-eye lens make us look macho & brooding
u especially: cute & moody
someone warned me u were hot & angsty
godfather to my queer children
rising unemployment of 16- to 18-year-olds in n. london
novitiates to this religious order
hairy crack hired to redecorate our lobby
don't hurt urself, yo-yo ma
damaged larynx can only whisper prophecies
gorilla costume being CELINE
bitch don't disrespect my savior
i never disparaged britney
go 3D-print urself a personality
artisans who sculpt bigger prick
to populate his celebrity profile
w. the pope u can never win
it's the outfits, i'm telling u

i was younger & more sexually adventurous
his appearance like monster
reverse nas: disease king
train so slow u ride the donkey
bend me over ~~man~~ person ray's pool table
insist on calling it
making love

坚持到底 TILL THE VERY END

"They take, as men are wont to do, with zeal"—A. Van Jordan

•

i pray for the ones underpaid & wanting to be slapped
the paramedics w/ shaky hands & hooks in mouths
interns w/ their lanyards, daddy issues & long duk dong

poets messy eaters b/c juice streaking down their chins
poets having good dental b/c always knocking teeth
poets extra tired b/c cocks asleep in jeans

poets improving their cardio b/c hearts swollen tight as fists
poets paying attention b/c—u know—kinda looking around
finding their way, tongues stiff like spit on a wick

trained pink palomino or safecracker's ear
hair shook loose like linguini
that busted-up cancer sack better not bother me

not here, not now
this band-aid wasn't made for our kind of flesh
the best part of brain surgery is everyone's guilty

the train may be delayed but a trip in the gravy boat is good for business
this cruise is gay, it's the real deal
u have to be lonely enough to slam tequila & raw-dawg it

i've considered the details, the quiet classy love-child
found under some branches, cute as a pumpkin
we were canoodling below deck when the weather girls jumped

pull in tighter, get us close
hover over the hotness if u can
how did u chip that tooth, minister

i remember:
save the best for last:
i'm from the government & i'm here to help

ACKNOWLEDGMENTS

his book is for Eric Issenberg

ratitude to:

Adam Day, for being a visionary

Paul Ritter, for the cover art / Robbie Myers, for connecting us

hank you to the editors of these journals & anthologies for their fine taste:

+doc, ANMLY, The Anstruther Reader: Ten Years of Poetry, Broadsides & Manifestos, Beloit Poetry Journal, Contemporary Verse 2 (CV2), Denver Quarterly, The Florida Review, Grist: A Journal of the Literary Arts, HAD, The Harvard Advocate, The Index, JAKE: The Anti-Literary Magazine, The Journal, Kestrel: A Journal of Literature & Art, Lana Turner: A Journal of Poetry & Opinion, Main Squeeze Magazine, The Malahat Review, Mercurius, Mercury Firs, Michigan Quarterly Review, Oyez Review, POETRY Magazine, Prelude, PRISM International, Reed Magazine, The Rumpus, The Southeast Review, The Spectacle, Sugar House Review, Swamp Ape Review, Tampa Review, Thayer, Thin Air, The Tiny, Volume Poetry, Water~Stone Review, Yalobusha Review

hanks, also, to my blurbers & readers, for sticking with me

MICHAEL CHANG

(they/them) is the author of *SYNTHETIC JUNGLE* (Northwestern University Press, 2023) & *THINGS A BRIGHT BOY CAN DO* (Coach House Books, 2025). They edit poetry at *Fence*.